Christian care series

When Addictions Threaten

Hope for Those Endangered by Addictions

Charles T. Knippel, Ph.D.

CPH.
SAINT-LOUIS

To

My Grandson,
Gregory James

1 2 3 4 5 6 7 8 9 10   09 08 07 06 05 04 03 02 01 00

Contents

Preface

Since the publication of my book *The Twelve Steps: The Church's Challenge and Opportunity*, I have envisioned a small book like this one as a companion for it.

In *The Twelve Steps*, I wrote about the origins of the Twelve-Step Spiritual Program of Recovery first formulated for Alcoholics Anonymous. I evaluated this program from a biblical perspective and offered recommendations for use of the twelve steps. In this present book about addictions I discuss various addictions for which twelve-step programs offer recovery and make recommendations for Christian care. My goal is to provide Christian perspectives on substance and behavior addictions and the care available for those endangered by addictions.

Like *The Twelve Steps*, this book is written for Christians, primarily from a biblical point of view. I have sought to make it brief but comprehensive, and both theologically and medically accurate without using technical jargon. I want this book to be helpful to professional caregivers as well as to any concerned person.

My pastoral experiences in the parish and my ministry in the areas of addictions and education convince me that addictions threaten to overtake all of us and even now enslave the lives of millions. They damage the lives of both addicted people and those others who are affected by their addictions. Many of these people are close to us and we care deeply about them. We very much want to give them good care and to take good care of ourselves. I hope this book will be helpful in carrying out this commitment.

As we consider addictions and how to care for people endangered by them, we are confident that God's rich health-giving resources are available for our task. We count on the Gospel of God's love in Jesus Christ. For the sake of Jesus' death that made good for our sins, God forgives our sinfulness and sin and the sinfulness and sin of all who trust in Jesus Christ as Savior and Lord. With his forgiveness he places his Holy Spirit into our lives. The Holy Spirit empowers us to overcome the enslaving control of sin and to live in the freedom of obedience to God. We sometimes, even often, falter and fail because of sin still at work in us. We have relapses. But we turn again and again to Jesus for forgiveness and new power to live more successfully in the freedom He gives. To be sure, in Jesus, God gives us and every Christian all we need to live as people who are secure in His love and dedicated to living the new life in Christ. This new life intends to set us free from all that hurts and harms life and to motivate us to love as He loves us.

Introduction

When we talk about addictions, we often focus on dependencies on drugs such as alcohol, marijuana, cocaine, heroin, and methamphetamine. Much has been written about chemical addictions, but today the term addiction has taken on larger meaning.

It wasn't too many years ago that the word "addiction" was used primarily, if not exclusively, to refer only to *drug* dependencies and to describe *physical* dependence on mind/mood altering drugs. Today, however, the word "addiction" has the larger meaning expressed by Anne Wilson Schaef and Diane Fassel in *The Addictive Organization*. Expanding the scope of concern, these authors view addiction as something more than physiological. They speak of addiction as having to do with processes (thoughts, attitudes, behaviors, and interactions) as well as substances. We can be addicted to

> any substance or process that has taken over our lives and over which we are powerless. It may or may not be a physiological addiction. An addiction is any process or substance that begins to have control over us in such a way that we feel we must be dishonest with ourselves or others about it.... The substance

addictions are ingestive: substances are taken into the body. All mood altering chemicals are addictive substances.... The concept of process addictions refers to a series of activities or interactions that "hook" a person, or on which a person becomes dependent. The common process addictions are work, sex, money, gambling, religion, relationships, and certain types of thinking. Actually, any process can be used addictively. For example, Schaef points out that even worry can be a process addiction. (pp. 57–58)

Howard Clinebell, argues for an enlarged definition of the addictions. In *Understanding and Counseling Persons with Alcohol, Drug, and Behavioral Addictions* (1998), he says:

Here, I follow the prevalent generic usage in much current writing that extends the term addiction beyond its original psychophysiological meaning to describe any obsessive-compulsive behavior in which there is some loss of voluntary control so that the victims seriously damage one or more important areas of their lives. (p. 24)

The broader use of the word "addiction" underscores the seriousness not only of substance addictions but also of a myriad of addictive behaviors that might otherwise be viewed as less serious than they actually are. This larger definition urges us to avoid tunnel vision and to give Christian attention to a vast array of both substance and process (or behavioral) addictions.

With a view to new understandings about addictions, how, then, can we define addiction? In his book *Addiction and Grace*, Gerald May gives this definition: "To define it directly, addiction is a state of compulsion, obsession, or preoccupation that enslaves a person's will and desire" (p. 14). An addicted person is one who has lost control of some aspect of living with the result that his entire life is out of control. The essence of every addiction is the addict's experience of powerlessness over a compulsive behavior that results in his life becoming unmanageable.

Many millions of people suffer because of their own addictions and/or those of others. The suffering concerns us because as Christians we share Jesus' interest in the quality of people's lives. He came to bring life in all its fullness, and by virtue of our baptism we participate in that commitment. Thus, it is important for us to be increasingly proficient in understanding and dealing with addictions that threaten to erode a vast number of human lives and threaten our own lives.

To enhance our ability to deal with addictions, I propose that we consider: 1) the addictive nature of the sinful human condition, 2) the addictions that sin generates, 3) the addiction of codependence, 4) Christian self-care in the world of addictions, and 5) Christian care for people addicted and disposed to addictions.

1

The Addictive Nature
of Sin

Why do people suffer from addictions? Is there something in the human condition that makes us prone to addictions? The Bible has an answer for these questions, and contemporary writers reflect the biblical response.

In *Codependence: Misunderstood—Mistreated* and *When Society Becomes an Addict*, Anne Wilson Schaef argues that a *generic addictive process* underlies all the various addictions and that it surrounds and influences all of us.

Keith Miller, in *Sin: Overcoming the Ultimate Deadly Addiction*, likewise discusses the addictive process, speaking of it explicitly in terms of sin. He shows that this blinding self-absorption

> called Sin—however well it may be disguised by our civilized exteriors—is the same elusive underlying dynamic as that in the life of the traditional chemical addict. Sin is the dynamic that leads addicts to fasten upon an addictive chemical or behavior that promises to fulfill their self-centered and often grandiose

dreams and to blot out the feelings that threaten to overwhelm them. (p. 52)

For Miller the underlying addictive process of which Schaef and Fassel speak is simply *sin* in human lives. Sin is our condition of separation from God (our inherited sinfulness) and our consequent acts of disobedience to God (our actual sins). Sin by its very nature moves us toward addictions; sin is addictive. The writer to the Hebrews speaks of "the sin that so easily entangles." He writes, "Therefore, since we are surrounded by such a great cloud of witnesses, let us throw off everything that hinders and the sin that so easily entangles, and let us run with perseverance the race marked out for us" (Heb. 12:1ff.). Sin moves us in the direction of bondage; it enslaves us. It propels us in the direction of loss of control over many "things of life" and many behaviors. This is the nature of sin. All Christians who experience addictions can identify with St. Paul when he says, "For what I want to do I do not do, but what I hate I do" (Rom. 7:15).

Jesus leads us to think about the addictiveness of sin in another way. He teaches that whoever would save his life will lose it (Matt. 16:25). Sin at work in us moves us in all the wrong directions to save our lives—to meet our deep and real needs as spiritual persons.

2

Addictions That Sin Generates

Addictions in General: Substance and Process

Addiction is a matter of loss of control over a substance or process. For example, a person who is addicted to alcohol can no longer consistently predict when he will begin drinking and, more significantly, when he will stop drinking. He has lost control over his use of alcohol. If a person's drinking, drug use, or behavior seriously harms one or more important areas of his life, and he continues his behavior, he is likely addicted and thus experiencing loss of control.

Enslaving addictions inevitably turn us away from God and from good. They are thieves that steal, kill, and destroy. Addictions generate, express, and foster idolatry. They become "gods" to those who pursue them.

Sin generates the many addictions that enslave us. Substances on which persons become addicted are alcohol and various kinds of other drugs. Common process addictions are related to work, sex, money, gambling, religion, organizations, shopping, relationships, certain types of thinking, worry, self-abuse, or acquiring money and power.

Substance Addictions

Various Kinds of Substance Addictions

Among substances we identify as addictive are alcohol, a variety of other mind- and mood-altering chemicals, including caffeine and nicotine, and food. Some stimulate the central nervous system. Others are depressants and hallucinogens. Still others have more than one kind of effect.

When we talk about substance addictions, we can speak of psychological addiction, physiological addiction, and psychological-physiological addiction. Some drugs like alcohol, cocaine, heroin, and nicotine are both psychologically and physiologically addicting. Perhaps drugs such as psilosybin and LSD are psychologically but not physiologically addicting. Then, too, some persons may become physiologically but not psychologically addicted to a drug. For example, someone may become physiologically addicted to morphine during a lengthy hospital stay, but not necessarily become psychologically addicted. Physiological addictions involve changes in a person's brain and body functions. To some degree, the same is likely true of some or all psychological and behavioral addictions. Research continually gives us new understandings about how addictions involve the whole person.

Food Addiction

Food-addicted people suffer from compulsive overeating. Many such people want to be free from their obsession with food. Often they use extreme and unhealthy means of dealing with their overeating or fear of overeating. They purge themselves after excessive eating or starve themselves.

A twelve-step group known as Overeaters Anonymous is devoted to helping people overcome their obsession with food and patterns of overeating. The group offers a recovery program for both the physical and spiritual aspects of compulsive eating.

To assist people in discovering whether or not they are compulsive overeaters, Overeaters Anonymous poses 15 questions which give an overview of the characteristics of addictive eating. These questions are as follows:

1. Do you eat when you're not hungry?

2. Do you go on eating binges for no apparent reason?

3. Do you have feelings of guilt and remorse after overeating?

4. Do you give too much time and thought to food?

5. Do you look forward with pleasure and anticipation to the time when you can eat alone?

6. Do you plan these secret binges ahead of time?

7. Do you eat sensibly before others and make up for it alone?

8. Is your weight affecting the way you live your life?

9. Have you tried to diet for a week (or longer), only to fall short of your goal?

10. Do you resent others telling you to "use a little willpower" to stop overeating?

11. Despite evidence to the contrary, have you continued to assert that you can diet "on your own" whenever you wish?

12. Do you crave to eat at a definite time, day or night, other than mealtime?

13. Do you eat to escape from worries or trouble?

14. Have you ever been treated for obesity or a food-related condition?

15. Does your eating behavior make you or others unhappy?

Of these questions Overeaters Anonymous says, "This series of questions may help you determine if you are a compulsive overeater. Many members of Overeaters Anonymous have found that they have answered yes to many of these questions"
(from www.overeatersanonymous.org/15quttxt.htm).

Process Addictions

Process addictions have to do with attitudes, behaviors, and interactions. They are unhealthy attachments to activities, thoughts, things, or people. As Keith Miller observes:

> Our attention can be captured this way by a chemical or other addictive substance, sex, gambling, or criminal habits. Or what we focus on can be something that is *good* in itself; it doesn't have to be a 'bad' thing. For instance, this focus may be on behavior, like work, or on another person, a mate, for instance, or a child, or it can be on religious programs or ourselves and our own ambitions. But whatever this unhealthy, compulsive attention is focused on, *that* is the controlling manifestation of our own particular Sin. (p. 111)

Work Addiction

Some process addictions are easily overlooked and need special attention because they are extremely damaging if not detected. One of these serious process addictions is addiction to work, sometimes referred to as workaholism. Wilson and Fassel express the opinion that workaholism may be the designer drug of the church as well as for the corporation. They view workaholism as an addictive process in which the addictive agent is work. The addict uses work to get ahead, achieve success, evade feeling, and ultimately avoid the joys of living.

The workaholic experiences an exhilarating adrenaline high and an increase in energy while busy at work. However, workaholism is ultimately physically and emotionally debilitating. It painfully affects the entire family and damages relationships both at home and work. When not planning his work or working, the work addict often experiences a sense of depression. He misses his "fix."

Robert W. Conroy, a psychiatrist formerly associated with The Menninger Clinic, describes work addiction as the addiction that is frequently deemed worthy of praise and imitation. He observes that hard workers are often viewed as mature, responsible, virtuous, and even patriotic. In the church, as well as in the corporate world, hard workers are seen as especially good and worthy of commendation.

However, Conroy makes clear that the person who loves work, feels gratified with accomplishment, and works hard to achieve a goal is not necessarily a work addict. Nor is the person who sometimes works overtime to meet a deadline or complete a project. The work addict is different; he thinks about work all the time. According to Conroy, the key element of work addiction is the inability to do without the excitement and stimulation of work.

Sex, Romance, Relationship Addiction

Sexual addiction expresses itself in a variety of ways. Sometimes the sex addict has trouble with just one process, sometimes with many. According to Anne Wilson Schaef in her book *Escape from Intimacy*, sexual addiction, like any other addiction, is mood-altering. Sexual obsession becomes a euphoric experience. The addiction is an obsession and total occupation with sex. The sex addict defines every relationship, indeed, everything sexually.

Sex addicts suffer serious consequences from their behavior. They lose relationships and have difficulties at work. Sometimes they are arrested, and they have financial problems. Over a period of time sex addicts lose interest in things that aren't sexual. They suffer from shame, low self-esteem, and self-hate. They experience a sense of hopelessness and despair.

There are different kinds of sex addicts. According to Schaef, some sex addicts are *romance* addicts. They are in love with the idea of romance. Schaef observes:

> The romance addict is in love with the idea of romance. The romance addict does not really care about the other person. The romance addict is also an expert in illusion, in fact, lives in illusion. For the romance addict, the belief that "some day my prince (or princess) will come," is not a fantasy. It is a real expectation. Romance addicts can also be addicted to causes and romantic (sometimes childishly "innocent") situations. (*Escape from Intimacy*, p. 47)

Among sex addicts, Schaef also identifies *relationship* addiction. Two main types of *relationship* addiction appear to foster intimacy but in reality avoid intimacy. In the first kind of relationship addiction, the person is addicted to having a relationship, real or fantasized. This person is "hooked" on the *idea* of relationship. In the second, a person is addicted to a relationship with a particular *person*.

Organization Addiction

As an expert in the field of process addictions, Schaef has much to say about organization addiction. One of her most challenging viewpoints is that organizations operate as an addictive substance in the lives of many people. The organization becomes the addictive agent for its employees. They become so attached to the promise of the mission of the organization that they are unwilling to pay attention to how the system is functioning. Schaef writes:

> The organization becomes an addictive substance when its actions are excused because of its lofty mission.... When organizations function as the addictive substance, it is in the interest to keep promoting the vision of the mission, because as long as the employees are hooked by it, they are unlikely to turn their awareness to the presence of discrepancies.... Loyalty to the organization becomes a fix when individuals become preoccupied with maintaining the organization.... When loyalty to the organization becomes a substitute for living one's own life, then the company has become the addictive substance of choice. (*Addictive Organization*, pp. 123–25)

In *The Christian Century* (January 3–10, 1990, pp. 18–21), Schaef published an article entitled, "Is the Church Addictive?" She calls upon the church to assess itself with a view to addictive processes.

Internet Addiction

A new addiction being discussed today is Internet addiction. Writing in *USA Today* (from www.addictions.org/netaddict.htm), Marilyn Elias reported a study, presented to the American Psychological Society, of 396 men and women online for an average of 38 hours a week. Of these 396 people Kimberly Young of the University of Pittsburgh-Bradford observed in a journal article that they were not just teenagers but many were middle-aged persons. They had lost control over their Internet usage and were unable to end it even though they suffered harmful effects in their personal and professional lives. Some lost friendships, jobs, spouses, and peace of mind.

Young named three rewards that drive Internet addiction: 1) Community—meeting people online, 2) Fantasy—adopting new personalities or playing out sexual fantasies, 3) Power-instant access to information and new people, a positive that can go bad.

Gambling Addiction

Gambling addiction is not new but is growing because of the availability of an increasing number of gambling casinos. Gambling addicts, like other addicts, are unable to control their behavior. They are preoccupied with gambling and unrelentingly pursue the "high" of winning. In turn, they suffer grave emotional, financial, and family problems. The suicide rate among pathological gamblers is higher than among drug addicted persons.

Gamblers Anonymous indicates the nature of gambling addiction by the content of the "20 Questions" it asks new members.

1. Did you ever lose time from work or school due to gambling?

2. Has gambling ever made your home life unhappy?

3. Did gambling affect your reputation?

4. Have you ever felt remorse after gambling?

5. Did you ever gamble to get money to pay debts or otherwise solve financial difficulties?

6. Did gambling cause a decrease in your ambition or efficiency?

7. After losing did you feel you must return as soon as possible and win back your losses?

8. After a win did you have a strong urge to return and win more?

9. Did you often gamble until your last dollar was gone?

10. Did you ever borrow to finance your gambling?

11. Have you ever sold anything to finance gambling?

12. Were you reluctant to use "gambling money" for normal expenditures?

13. Did gambling make you careless of the welfare of yourself or your family?

14. Did you ever gamble longer than you had planned?

15. Have you ever gambled to escape worry or trouble?

16. Have you ever committed, or considered committing, an illegal act to finance gambling?

17. Did gambling cause you to have difficulty in sleeping?

18. Do arguments, disappointments or frustrations create within you an urge to gamble?

19. Did you ever have an urge to celebrate any good fortune by a few hours of gambling?

20. Have you ever considered self-destruction or suicide as a result of your gambling?

With regard to these questions, Gamblers Anonymous concludes that if a person answers "yes" to seven or more of these questions, that person may have a gambling addiction problem.

Characteristics of Addiction

All addictions have characteristics in common. They are attempts on the part of the addicted to deal with inborn personal and interpersonal human needs. These are false solutions to our deepest and truest human needs, rooted in our most essential need for a right relationship with God and His people. Addictions certainly show how, apart from the intervention of God, we seek to find our lives and lose them in the attempt.

Many specific characteristics of addicted persons are identified by professionals in the field of addictions. They describe addicts as self-centered, dishonest, and perfectionistic people who are in denial about their addiction. They are defensive and fearful. They blame others for their misery and have a strong need to control and manipulate persons and events. Their thinking processes are abnormal and their feelings are frozen. Addicts experience depression and stress and ultimately become spiritually, ethically, and financially bankrupt.

3

The Addiction
of Codependence

Definition of Codependence

A̶ddiction and codependence are usually described as different phenomena. However, codependence is also characterized as an addiction. Sharon Wegscheider-Cruse speaks of codependence as an addiction to another person or persons and their problems or to a relationship and its problems. In *Codependence Misunderstood—Mistreated*, Anne Wilson Schaef comments:

> I would like to suggest that what we are calling codependence is, indeed, a *disease* that has many forms and expressions and that grows out of a disease process that is inherent in the system in which we live. I call this disease process the *addictive process*. (p. 25)

Howard Clinebell observes that codependents are "caregiving persons who are dependent on addicted people's dependence," dedicated to "'helping' the addicted by attempting to control them, protecting them from the painful consequences of their actions, and taking responsibility for their destructive behavior" (1998, p. 26).

Schaef describes a codependent as a person who is involved in an emotionally close relationship with an addict, had at least an addicted parent or grandparent, and/or grew up in an emotionally repressive family. Melody Beattie writes in *Codependent No More*, "A codependent person is one who has let someone else's behavior affect him or her and is obsessed with controlling other people's behavior" (p. 31). In his article, "Letting Go of Codependency," Edmund J. Bourne defines codependency as follows:

> [It is] the tendency to put others' needs before your own. You accommodate to others to such a degree that you to tend to discount or ignore your own feelings, desires and basic needs. Your self-esteem depends largely on how well you please, take care of and/or solve problems for someone else (or many others). The consequence of maintaining a codependent approach to life is a lot of resentment, frustration and unmet personal needs. When these feelings and needs remain unconscious, they often resurface as anxiety—especially chronic, generalized anxiety. The long-term effects of codependency are enduring stress, fatigue, burnout and eventually serious physical illness. (from www.npadnews.com/co-dep.htm)

Characteristics of Codependence

Codependency is a style of living shaped and maintained, in large degree, by dysfunctional rules within the family or a larger social system. These rules impede healthy growth and make personal change difficult, if not impossible. Among these rules are the following injunctions: "don't feel," "don't talk," "don't trust," "don't be selfish," "don't play or have fun," and, above all, "be perfect."

Codependent persons are overly responsible. They feel responsible for life's problems and taking care of others. They have an intense drive to control the behavior of others with guilt and manipulation. In turn, they have a sense of low self-esteem and self-worth; they feel ashamed of themselves and put others first in their lives to their own detriment. Whatever feelings of self-worth they may have come from helping others. Interpersonal relationships are difficult for codependents. They have difficulty trusting others, knowing what is normal in life, and asking for what they need from others. They tend to fear abandonment and seek love from people who are unable to give it to them. Many codependents marry alcoholics and other addicts. Some become alcoholics and suffer from a variety of addictions.

The life of the codependent is filled with pain. To deal with this pain, codependents often enter the helping professions and work with people for all the wrong reasons.

4

Self-Care in the World of Addictions

Addictions threaten all society, including the people of God and their pastors. Like others, the people of God and their pastors are not strangers to addictions to alcohol and other substances. Nor are they strangers to addictions to work, sex, food, gambling, and unhealthy relationships.

We need to concern ourselves with both prevention and recovery. Both begin with learning about addictions and the process of recovery.

Chemical addiction, primarily alcoholism, provides us with a paradigm for understanding not only drug addiction but other addictions. If we know about the nature and progression of chemical addiction and the road to recovery, we will know much about all kinds of addictions and how to recover from them.

The Nature and Progression of Chemical Addiction

Chemical dependency is more than the abuse of chemicals. It is a condition that is characterized by the loss of control over the use of one or more chemicals.

Because of the loss of control phenomenon, the chemically dependent person cannot predict with consistency when he will use his drug/s of choice and how extensive the use will be. This means the person cannot consistently predict when his drug use will begin and when it will stop. This loss of control factor is widely regarded as an illness or disease. Christianity aptly calls this a "sin-illness." It is an psychological/physical illness that is born out of sinfulness and involves the sins of chemical abuse and intoxicated behavior.

Chemical dependency is a progressive and ultimately fatal condition for which there is no known cure. However, resources for recovery do exist and a sober way of life is possible through abstinence from mind-altering chemicals.

A great deal is known about how chemical dependency progresses. Charts have been developed to provide a profile of the downward progression of the sin-illness, the identified stages, and steps. The best-known of these charts is "A Tentative Chart of Alcohol Addiction and Recovery 1962." The first edition was crafted by M. M. Glatt in 1954 on the basis of research done by E. M. Jellinek of Yale University (Clinebell, 1968, p. 231).

Glatt's chart describes the progression of alcohol addiction in three phases—the *prodromal* (or early), the *crucial* (or middle), and the *chronic* (or late). The *prodromal* phase is the introductory phase characterized by problem drinking but not loss-of-control drinking. It begins with occasional relief drinking and proceeds to constant relief drinking. This phase consists of an increase in alcohol tolerance, the onset of memory blackouts (lapses), hidden drinking, increasing dependence on alcohol, repeated drunken driving, urgency of first drinks, and increasing memory blackouts.

The second phase is termed *crucial* because it is very important that the addicted person seek recovery during this phase. Lasting recovery is rarely achieved during the chronic phase.

The crucial phase begins with the loss of control that marks the onset of addiction and signals that a person can no longer return to social drinking. Glatt identifies the steps of this phase as: drinking bolstered with excuses, grandiose and aggressive behavior, persistent remorse, failures at efforts to control drinking, the failure of promises and resolutions, attempts at geographical escapes, loss of other interests, avoidance of family and friends, work and money troubles, unreasonable resentments, neglect of food, loss of ordinary will power, tremors and early morning drinks, and decreasing alcohol tolerance.

The *chronic* phase is introduced by the onset of lengthy intoxications and progresses with moral deterioration, impaired thinking, indefinable fears, drinking with people from a lower social class, and suicide attempted or completed. Then follows inability to initiate action, obsessions with drinking, vague spiritual desires, the exhaustion of all alibis, and the admission of complete defeat.

Many charts of addictions have been created on the basis of the Glatt's chart. Among them are charts for gambling, codependence, overeating, and cocaine addiction.

The very nature of the illness makes it difficult for an addict to recognize his condition. Even though the addict may sometimes feel guilt and shame, he uses self-protecting defense mechanisms, such as denial, rationalization, and projection. As an intrinsic facet of his illness, the addicted person denies that he has a problem and thus fails to see the relationship between his addiction and the apparent problems in his life. In turn, he reasons that he does not use drugs more than others and that any problems he may have are of little significance. Finally, he blames others for his drug use and for whatever problems people accuse him of having or causing.

A Christian Perspective

The addicted person instinctively seeks to protect his addictive behavior because he views his addictive substance or process as essential to his well-being. *It is only when the pain of compulsive behavior becomes greater than the pleasure derived from it that the addicted person will be open to help for recovery.* At that moment he discovers the inability of his own will-power to bring about recovery. He recognizes his powerlessness over his addiction and that his whole life has become unmanageable. Without help, addicted persons can only despair. They will continue in their addiction, commit suicide, die as a result of their substance abuse, or lose their sanity. With help, addicted persons can and do recover.

It is wrong to say that a Christian who becomes addicted to a life-destroying substance or process is no longer a Christian. Because addiction involves loss of control, the addict's misuse of substances and processes can be viewed as a sin of weakness rather than a deliberate and persistent sin that immediately destroys faith. This does not mean that addictive behaviors are not dangerous to faith. They are. They are idolatrous behaviors that both weaken and threaten Christian faith. But no matter how weak Christian faith may become, it is nonetheless saving faith as long as it exists, for faith is the Holy Spirit's very own saving gift in Baptism. However, it is most certainly true that the Christian who continues in his addiction runs the grave risk of losing his faith. Pursuing his addiction to "save his life," he increasingly looks to it or them as his "god." He runs the very real risk of thrusting God's saving presence from his life. Jesus' words apply, "For whoever wants to save his life will lose it, but whoever loses his life for me will find it" (Matt. 16:25).

Means of Recovery

It is just as difficult for Christians as for others to discern addictions at work in their lives. This is why we need to monitor our lives very carefully and act for recovery when we detect any hint of an addiction at work, especially when others express concern about our possible addictive behavior.

Certainly God makes it possible for us to confront our addictions because Christ has taken our sin upon Himself, suffered our punishment by his death on the cross, and has continued to accept us as His very own. God's forgiveness, for Jesus' sake, makes it possible for us to speak the truth in love to ourselves and seek His help.

For many addicted persons, medical and psychological help are important and necessary. The vast majority of persons who recover from addictions do so by using the recovery process outlined in the Twelve-Step Spiritual Program of Recovery.[1] Although this program was originally designed for the recovery of alcoholics and is not explicitly Christian, it can be modified and employed with Christian understandings.

From our Christian viewpoint, these steps must be understood and used from a biblical perspective. Similar to the Christian adaptation of the Twelve Steps offered in my previous book, I offer here a Christian version of the Twelve Steps. This version recognizes that we are made right with God only through faith in his forgiveness for sins that has been made possible by the saving death and resurrection of Jesus Christ. In turn, it acknowledges that we are able to work the Twelve Steps only through the power of the Holy Spirit who transforms the lives of all forgiven persons.

Because God has endowed us with repentance to know and confess our sins and to trust in Jesus Christ for the forgiveness of sins and renewal of life, we are able to:

1. Admit that we are sinners as well as forgiven and renewed people. We daily sin much and often find ourselves powerless over facets of our lives that are not under the control of the Holy Spirit and that dishonor God and hurt us and others.

2. Believe that God can and does daily forgive our sins for Jesus' sake and liberate and renew our lives through the work of the Holy Spirit.

3. Live daily under the Holy Spirit's power and, in the promise and new life of Holy Baptism, daily turn our will and our lives over to the care of God and His recreating power and make fuller use of His gift of the Holy Spirit for the renewal of facets of our lives that need transformation.

4. Make a searching and fearless inventory of our sinful behaviors that require immediate attention.

5. Admit to ourselves, to God, and at least one other Christian the exact nature of our sins. Mindful of the comforting and reassuring benefits of individual absolution, we value the privilege of making

private confession before the pastor and receiving holy absolution from God through him.

6. Be ready to have God remove our sinful behavior.

7. Humbly ask Him to remove our sinful behavior.

8. Make a list of all persons we have harmed, and be willing to make amends to them all.

9. Make direct amends to such people wherever possible, except when to do so would injure them or others.

10. Continue day by day to take a personal inventory and when we sin, promptly admit our sin, receive God's forgiveness and life-renewing power, and respond in responsible Christian ways.

11. Use God's Word and the Lord's Supper to enrich our relationship with God, as well as use God's Word and prayer to discover a clearer understanding of God's will that the Holy Spirit enables us to carry out.

12. Carry the message of the saving and freeing Gospel of Jesus Christ to people who need God's life-transforming resources to deal with a variety of concerns and, finally, to seek to express our growing Christian maturity in all aspects of life.

Perhaps an illustration can show how to use the adapted Twelve Steps for intentional, goal-directed Christian growth. Think of yourself as a codependent person. You often feel inferior to others and devalue yourself. Out of anger and depression, you try to feel and appear better by controlling other people, taking advantage of them, and "putting them down." When you cannot control others, you feel even worse about yourself. This, of course, is not the way you want to be. In fact, you sense that as a Christian you have good reasons to value yourself much more than you do. Your goal is to value yourself as God values you because of Christ.

What can you do to achieve your goal? In brief, admit that of yourself you are powerless over your attitude of poor self-esteem. Recognize that your heavenly Father wants you to know your true worth as his child. He stands ready to forgive your faulty perceptions and actions and to change your attitudes and behavior. Therefore, intentionally turn yourself over to the care of God, confessing your sins of belittling yourself and hurting others. Ask God to take away your low self-esteem and resulting hurtful behaviors. Recall from his Word the forgiving love he has for you in Christ. Be assured that Christ has paid for your sins and that God forgives also your sins of self-depreciation and the misuse of others and that he values you highly as his very own possession. Ask another person, perhaps your pastor, to hear your confession and announce to you God's forgiveness for the particular sins with which you are dealing.

As you rely on God for help, his full forgiveness for Jesus' sake will truly comfort you and empower you toward overcoming your sins of thinking little of yourself and of treating others badly in an attempt to feel better. By the Gospel God will enable you more closely to reach your goals to have healthier esteem for yourself and others and to struggle successfully more often than not against the temptation to devalue and abuse yourself and others. You may take one step forward toward your goal, or several, only to fall back; but you continue to practice the steps. Christian growth is a lifelong process.

As God's love reaches deeply into your life, you may want to make amends to people you have hurt. God himself enables such amends-making and through it heals damaged relationships and blesses us with a sense of integrity.

This is simply one illustration of how a Christian understanding of the Twelve Steps might aid in practicing intentional, goal-directed Christian growth. We can apply these same principles to the misuse of drugs, food, money, sex, and power. The Christianized Steps can help us deal with any sin that readily entangles us: bad temper, impatience, jealously, hatred, or selfish ambition. (pp. 88–91)

A Christian who chooses to practice the Twelve-Step Program to recover from an addiction may find it helpful to join a mutual help group made up of people who are struggling with the same addiction. Within that fellowship he can practice the Twelve Steps as a Christian and receive support and encouragement.

There are times when Christians intent on recovery will find it beneficial to place themselves under the care of competent medical and mental health professionals. To facilitate their recovery they can choose to participate in a residential or out-client addictions treatment program. It is imperative for God's people to recognize their need and seek adequate treatment for recovery.

Dealing with Codependency

Special attention to Codependency is appropriate since the lives so many millions are affected by addicted persons.

Individual Codependency

In the article entitled, "Letting Go of Codependency," Dr. Edmund Bourne focuses on codependents as individuals and offers some suggestions about recovery from codependence that we can give Christian meaning. He writes:

> Recovering from codependency in essence involves learning to love and take care of yourself. It means giving at least equal time to your own needs as well as those of others. It means setting limits on how much you will do tolerate and learning to say "no" when appropriate. (from www.npadnews.com/co-dep.htm)

Bourne's suggestions have special value when we view them within the context of a faith relationship with God through Jesus Christ. We are able to commit ourselves to doing what Bourne recommends because of the acceptance, encouragement, and new life that God gives us as He daily forgives our sins on account of Jesus' saving life and sacrificial death for all sinners on the cross. In Christ, God offers and gives us what we need for victorious living—security, significance, enablement, and a healthy perspective about ourselves and others. We remember that Jesus directs us to love our neighbors as we love ourselves. When we rightly regard and love ourselves as persons loved by God, we are better able to love others.

Al-Anon is a twelve-step mutual-help fellowship that offers help for codependent persons. Sponsored by Al-Anon, Alateen is a fellowship that gives care and support to teenage codependents.

Family Codependency

It is not only the addicted individual who needs help for recovery but that person's entire family as well. The whole family suffers because of an addictive illness. Thus the whole family needs aid and assistance to deal with their current crisis and to experience long-term, growth-producing recovery. Treatment centers and other agencies offer whole-family care and counseling for codependent families. They invite families, or as many members of the family who are willing, to participate in their recovery programs.

Dealing with Work Addiction

Work addiction affects the lives of a vast number of people. Among them are members of the clergy who rightly want to be wholly dedicated to their calling.

An article, "Six Steps Out of Work Addiction," printed by Scott Publishing, Inc., in *Personal Health Letter,* suggests answers to the question, "What's the cause for work addiction?"

> Many people put in long hours on the job. Some are able to balance their dedication to work with an equally rich personal life, making plenty of time for family, friends and play. Others become addicted to work. Unable to achieve a healthy balance, workaholics often have trouble feeling "alive" unless they're working.

> You can consider yourself work addicted if you: prefer work to play or social events, look forward to holidays as you can use time to get ahead on work projects, resist taking vacations, often eat meals while working, and spend most of your waking time working.

> People who work long hours with little time for other activity may suffer from a host of ailments: stress, anxiety, depression, fatigue, headaches and gastrointestinal problems. They eventually become less productive and efficient and develop a distorted view of goals and needs.

> Loving your work is great, but if you see signs of addiction learn ways to create a sensible balance, for example:

Gradually cut back the overtime hours you work beyond your normal work week. Get to a point where you don't work evenings or weekends.

Work smarter, not harder. This could mean delegating work to others or skipping unimportant tasks.

Cancel family or social commitments only if unavoidable.

Methodically schedule leisure activities until they become routine.

When you're away from work try to keep your thoughts on the activity at hand.

Don't feel guilty about not working. You deserve a break. And the change of pace will leave you refreshed for your return to work. (p. 8)

Many people, of course, including pastors, cannot escape working evenings and weekends. Nevertheless, they can find many of these suggestions extremely helpful and adapt them to their particular lifestyle.

5

Christian Care for People Addicted and Subject to Addictions

Christian Care for Those Subject to Addictions

Causes of Addictions

An increasing amount of research points to the probability that a significant number of addicts not only have a dependency—encouraging environment but an inherited predisposition toward particular addictions as well. Strong evidence exists that this is especially the case among alcoholics. A predisposition, of course, does not mean inevitability.

The causality of addictions involves spiritual factors for many if not most addicts. By using an addictive substance or process, many addicts look for and believe they have found a way of overcoming their sense of alienation from God (or their "Higher Power") and other people and from their personal feelings of insignificance and insecurity. In reality, however, whatever they experience is simply the result of altered minds. But for a time they seem convinced that they have found a genuine solution to unmet and deeply felt personal and spiritual needs. This is their conviction as long as they derive benefits from their addiction that they believe they cannot obtain elsewhere.

However, no matter what part the attempt to fulfill spiritual needs plays in the *causality* of addictions, *the religious search becomes intrinsic to the illness as it progresses.* In the same way that the addict uses his substance or process to cause problems, he uses the same substance or process to solve his problems. He does not realize that they can be authentically solved only within a faith relationship with God in Christ. Nor does he look to God for the genuine help he so desperately needs.

This view is supported by the premise of Clinebell, that "alcohol provides a pseudosatisfaction for the alcoholic's religious needs." In *Understanding and Counseling the Alcoholic* he writes that "the alcoholic thus seeks to satisfy his religious needs by nonreligious means" (p. 73). In his latest book on alcohol, drug, and behavioral addictions, Clinebell adds, "Any in-depth understanding of chemical dependencies and other addictions must include the recognition that many addicted persons are attempting to meet religious hungers by alcohol, other psychoactive drugs, or addictive behaviors" (p. 267).

Prevention: The Gospel, the Church, and Christian Education

Clinebell's premise strongly supports the Christian conviction that the Gospel and the Christian fellowship are the basic and essential resources for the prevention of addictions. Addictions destroy life, but through the Gospel Jesus gives life. In turn, the Christian community is a fellowship of believers who strengthen one another's faith and life in Christ. In this fellowship, as we live under the Gospel, we give and receive love, support, and encouragement. Such care equips us in the struggle against addictions that threaten to enslave us.

Education within the Christian fellowship is a vital part of the prevention task. We have many opportunities to educate and learn about addictions that threaten us and how to confront them. We can use sermons, Bible classes, study groups, organization discussions, workshops, tracts, and caring conversations.

Christian Care for Addicted People

Purposes and Approaches

Statistics suggest that many people in our congregations and communities suffer from addictions to substances and processes. Quite possibly many of the troubled and troublesome people in Christian congregations are people affected by addictions. In turn, many are disturbed and disturbing because they are dealing with codependence, itself a serious addiction. This understanding in itself may help us relate more patiently and helpfully to difficult persons. As Edwin Freedman reminds us *in Generation to Generation*, troublesome people in the congregation are most often people who have unresolved personal and family issues (pp. 35–39, 193–219).

Our goal for giving care to addicted persons is to enable them by the Gospel to have a strong faith relationship with God in Christ, to be free from their addictions, and to live joyful and fulfilling lives of obedience to God and of service to all in need of God's love. Most assuredly, we want them to be confident in the forgiveness of all their sins through faith in Jesus Christ as their Savior from sin and possess a certain hope of eternal life in heaven where God will deliver them, and all Christians, from all sins and sinful behaviors forever.

As we shape Christian care for an addicted person, we need to recognize that when an addicted person seeks help from the church for addiction-related issues, he is frequently coerced by others to make the contact. He may feel anger toward God, other people, and the clergy about past disappointments, real or imagined. This suggests that all of us, both pastors and congregation members, who give care need to build a relationship of trust, notably by showing interest in the addict's personal view of his situation. We will wisely begin by listening to the suffering person about his understandings and attitudes and move from there. We will focus on aiding the addicted person to learn about addictions, to recognize and accept his addiction(s), and to obtain treatment.

Our entire care relationship with the addicted person requires that we strive caringly and carefully to speak the truth in love. When it is appropriate in the progress of the care relationship, we are to use the Bible's Law and Gospel messages in loving ways. We are to speak in ways that enable the person in pain to lower his defenses and hear what God has to say so that the Holy Spirit can do His work.

Addicted persons who reach out for help are usually fearful, guilt-ridden, and self-condemning. Generally, they are experiencing physical, emotional, and spiritual pain. Thus, by speaking the truth in love, we focus on not being judgmental but on using Law statements to help the addict understand why his life is chaotic. We show the suffering person that his addiction is destroying his relationship with God and that his entire life is in opposition to God's will and under God's judgment because of his addiction.

Then, so that he does not despair but has hope for recovery, we speak the Gospel of God's forgiving love and help in Jesus Christ again and again at various times in the relationship and in various ways. We communicate the Gospel as God's very own way of producing repentance and conveying the forgiveness of sins with all its reconciling, comforting, and life-changing power.

Since an addiction is a loss-of-control condition that affects the person physically, mentally, emotionally, and socially, as well as spiritually, we properly encourage addicted persons to obtain the multidisciplinary treatment suitable for the particular addiction(s). This is a high priority because we want the addicts to recover and because only recovering persons who are able to hear and think clearly are able to hear the fullness of our Law/Gospel messages.

Treatment Possibilities

Addiction treatment centers are readily available in most areas. They provide residential and outpatient treatment opportunities for both the addicted and their family members who also desperately need recovery. In addition, addiction treatment centers are readily available in most areas. They provide residential and outpatient treatment opportunities for both the addicted and their family members who also desperately need recovery. In addition, supportive mutual-help groups offer recovery assistance for those who enter treatment centers as well as for those who do not. For some persons participation in a supportive group will in itself be the treatment of choice.

Whether persons enter medical treatment or choose to participate in the fellowship of an appropriate support group, it behooves us to provide ongoing care and the fellowship of the Christian community.

Confrontation/Intervention

Many addicted people do not readily recognize their need to alter facets of their life-style. They do not normally take the initiative to reach out for help. Others know that they need to make changes in their lives but are hesitant for a variety of reasons to reach out for help. However, there are effective ways of helping addicted persons acknowledge and accept their need for treatment.

To guide us we have the words of Jesus in Matthew 18: "If your brother sins against you, go and show him his fault, just between the two of you. If he listens to you, you have won your brother over. But if he will not listen, take one or two others along, so that every matter may be established by the testimony of two or three witnesses." Also we recall the words of St. Paul, "Brothers, if someone is caught in a sin, you who are spiritual should restore him gently" (Galatians 6:1).

It is essential to speak the truth of both the Law and Gospel in love in very special situations—to those who will not reach out for help. This is a direct confrontation with the addicted person.

In his book *Basic Types of Pastoral Care and Counseling*, Howard Clinebell says something very helpful about confrontation.

> Confrontation is an indispensable skill.... The central goal of confronting anyone is to enable self-con-

frontation—i.e., to help them face the behavior that hurts themselves and/or others and to feel guilt that therefore is appropriate. (p. 142)

Next, Clinebell explains how confrontation is most likely to be successful. He uses the "speaking the truth in love" concept.

Confrontation is most likely to result in self-confrontation when it includes two aspects. These are expressed well in New Testament language as "speaking the truth in love" (Eph. 4:15, referred to earlier as the "growth formula"). Speaking the truth is most effective when it is done in the context of caring love. Honest confrontation, after some trust is established, usually strengthens counseling relationships, rather than weakening them. (p. 144)

Often we are reluctant to confront others. However, when we confront *in love* we are more comfortable in speaking the truth and others are more capable of non-defensively hearing what we have to say. It is vitally important for us to let the persons whom we confront know that we care about them, that we want to share with them something that is important in our relationship with them, and then be willing to let them respond initially in defensive ways without rejecting them. "I messages" are of great value in the task of confrontation—the kind of "I messages" we will review when we talk about the steps of team intervention.

Often we carry out our confrontation alone, one-on-one. However, when an individual being confronted does not respond positively to *one* caring person, Jesus tells us that others should join in the confrontation effort. In the field of addictions we refer to this kind of confrontation as team intervention. Vernon Johnson, founder of the Johnson Institute, gave advice about this kind of intervention in his book *Intervention—How to Help Someone Who Doesn't Want Help*. In this little volume he discusses the gathering of an intervention team, the gathering of data, rehearsal of the intervention, finalizing details, and carrying out an intervention. The recommendations that follow feature some of his suggestions.

The first step in intervention is for the concerned individual or individuals to make a list of meaningful persons in the life of the person to be confronted and then to form an intervention team of three or four or more persons. Those on the team may be the person's employer or supervisor, spouse, parents, children, friends and neighbors, coworkers, and perhaps a pastor. Whoever participates should have firsthand knowledge of the addictive behavior. In turn, the team needs a coordinator, an addictions counselor or someone else with experience in intervention.

Gathering the data is the second step. Members of the team are to prepare written lists of specific incidents or conditions related to the person's behavior. Each item should explicitly describe a particular incident and be formulated as an "I message." Typically these "I messages" involve a statement of a team member's observation of the addict's behavior at a specific time, his feelings about that behavior, and the effects of that behavior on him.

In an intervention a person might say to an alcoholic "Last Friday when you came home from work it was evident you had been drinking. You stumbled into the house and fell over the coffee table. You broke an expensive vase. I picked you up and put you in bed. Then I cleaned up your mess. I was scared; you could barely walk and you had driven home. I was also angry with you for all the commotion you caused." To a food addict an intervener might say, "On Thanksgiving Day you binged on everything available including several desserts. Before we even got up from the table, you immediately excused yourself and went to the bathroom. I followed you; from outside the door I heard you purging. I apologized to our friends and relatives about your abrupt behavior. I told them that you had a touch of the flu. I felt embarrassed that I had to make excuses for your behavior. I was angry and disgusted, but at the same time I was very worried about your condition."

It is imperative for members of the intervention team to check out treatment options, even make advance treatment arrangements. Then they rehearse the intervention. Johnson suggests the following: 1) designate a chairperson; 2) go over each item on the written lists that team members have prepared; 3) determine the order in which the team members will read their lists during the intervention; 4) choose someone to play the role of the person to be confronted; 5) determine the responses that team members will make to the confronted person.

Johnson suggests that the intervention session be introduced with words similar to these: "John, we're here because we care about you and want to help. This is going to be difficult for you and for us, but one of the requests I have is that you give us the chance to talk and promise to listen, even though listening may be difficult. Will you help us by listening?"

There are many more issues that need to be considered in doing intervention, but these suggestions give some ideas about how the process works. For more information, I recommend Johnson's book or a person knowledgeable about addictions and intervention.

Mutual Conversation and Support

In Holy Baptism God in His goodness has made us members of the Christian Church, the very Body of Christ. As members of Christ's Church, we are to represent Christ to one another and to those outside the fellowship. God wants us to be members of a cared for and caring fellowship. Perhaps the resource among those mentioned by Dr. Luther that we often forget to employ to its fullest and fail to use energetically is the mutual conversation and consolation of brethren. God would have us be members of a cared for and caring fellowship, the very Body of Christ (the church). Often others, not knit together by our Lord Jesus, seem to have a greater appreciation than we of mutual aid and support relationships among people with common concerns. We can point to the fellowships of Alcoholics Anonymous, Al-Anon, Narcotics Anonymous, Cocaine Anonymous, Parents Anonymous, Emotions Anonymous, Overeaters Anonymous, Gambler's Anonymous and many more.

These groups give us reason to re-evaluate what we have as Christians who are related to one another as members of the Body of Christ for the purpose of mutual care. We have the fellowship in which we are able to do what St. Paul describes: "Speaking the truth in love, we will in all things grow up into him who is the Head, that is Christ" (Ephesians 4:15). Indeed, as St. Paul has written, "God has combined the members of the body and has given greater honor to the parts that lacked it, so that there should be no division in the body, but that its parts should have equal concern for each other. If one part suffers, every part suffers with it; if one part is honored, every part rejoices with it" (1 Corinthians 12:24–26).

My recommendation is that we work energetically to foster and maintain mutual-help support groups among Christians within the context of the Church where we work intensively to develop relationships of openness and trust and assist each other in overcoming particular problems and growing in the Christian fait and life. Within such fellowships we should seriously consider using a Bible-based Christian version of the Twelve Steps. Using such a program, we can aid one another to overcome loss-of-control behaviors.

Conclusion

Addictions threaten us and others. Sin is a fact of life, and sin is addictive. Sin generates a large variety of addictions. We can become addicted to any and every substance and process. But God has provided us with physical and spiritual resources for caring for ourselves and others when addictions threaten. Most important of all, we have the assurance of the forgiveness of sins from a gracious God who made his Son to be sin for us. We are God's very own through the saving faith that God has given us in Baptism and strengthens in us through His Word and the Lord's Supper. It is faith that trusts Jesus' saving work for our salvation here and hereafter. And the same God who gives us faith and forgives us also empowers us by His Holy Spirit to know and strive to do His gracious will for His honor, for our good, and for the good others. He places us among His people to share in the benefits of mutual care.

With the goodness of God in mind, we remember once again the words of the writer to the Hebrews that so powerfully speak to our concerns about addictions that threaten. To us and to all Christians, he writes:

Let us throw off everything that hinders and the sin that so easily entangles and let us run with perseverance the race marked out for us. Let us fix our eyes on Jesus, the author and perfecter of our faith, who for the joy set before him endured the cross, scorning the shame, and sat down at the right hand of the throne of God. Consider him who endured such opposition from sinful men, so that you will not grow weary, and lose heart. (Hebrews 12:1–3)

Here are most certainly words to live by in a world where addictions threaten. They are words of hope and encouragement rooted in God's love in Christ. "Let us fix our eyes on Jesus, the author and perfecter of our faith."

Footnote

1. In *Alcoholics Anonymous* (New York: Alcoholics Anonymous World Services, Inc., 1976; pp. 58–59), Bill Wilson states the Twelve Steps. This program needs special Christian attention because it was formulated for people of various beliefs and no belief to effect an intrapersonal dynamic that produces an abstinent way of life. For wide acceptance in a pluralistic society, the program speaks of God as the "Higher Power" and as "God *as we understand him.*" Furthermore, it suggests that a relationship with God is possible apart from Jesus Christ. The original twelve steps are as follows:

> Remember that we deal with alcohol—cunning, baffling, powerful! Without help it is too much for us. But there is One who has all power—that one is God. Half measures availed us nothing. We stood at the turning point. We asked his protection and care with complete abandon.

Here are the steps we took, which are suggested as a Program of Recovery.

1. We admitted we were powerless over alcohol—that our lives had become unmanageable.

2. Came to believe that a Power greater than ourselves could restore us to sanity.

3. Made a decision to turn our will and our lives over to the care of God *as we understood him.*

4. Made a searching and fearless moral inventory of ourselves.

5. Admitted to God, to ourselves, and to another human being the exact nature of our wrongs.

6. Were entirely ready to have God remove all these defects of character.

7. Humbly asked him to remove our shortcomings.

8. Made a list of all persons we had harmed, and became willing to make amends to them all.

9. Made direct amends to such people wherever possible, except when to do so would injure them or others.

10. Continued to take personal inventory and when we were wrong promptly admitted it.

11. Sought through prayer and meditation to improve our conscious contact with God *as we understood Him*, praying only for knowledge of his will for us and the power to carry that out.

12. Having had a spiritual awakening as the result of these steps, we tried to carry this message to alcoholics, and to practice these principles in all our affairs.

The Twelve Steps and a brief excerpt from the text *Alcoholics Anonymous,* 3rd Edition, are reprinted with permission of Alcoholics Anonymous World Services, Inc. (A.A.W.S.). Per-

Books for
Additional Reading

Ackerman, Robert J. *Let Go and Grow: Recovery for Adult Children*. Pompano Beach, FL: Health Communcations, Inc., 1987.

Beattie, Melody. *Beyond Codependency: And Getting Better All The Time*. New York: Harper/Hazelden, 1989.

_____. *Codependent No More*. San Francisco: Harper and Row, Publishers, 1987.

Black, Claudia. *Children of Alcoholics: It Will Never Happen to Me*. New York: Ballentine Books, 1981.

Clinebell, Howard J. *Understanding and Counseling the Alcoholic through Religion and Psychology*. Nashville: Abingdon Press, 1968.

_____. *Understanding and Counseling Persons with Alcohol, Drug, and Behavioral Addictions*. Rev. and enl. ed. Nashville: Abingdon Press, 1998.

Friedman, Edwin H., *Generation to Generation: Family Process in Church and Synagogue*. New York: The Guilford Press, 1985.

Johnson, Vernon E. *Intervention: How to Help Someone Who Doesn't Want Help*. Minneapolis: Johnson Institute Books, 1986.

Kinney, Jean and Leaton, Gwen. *Loosening the Grip: A Handbook of Alcohol Information*. 5th ed. St. Louis: Mosby, 1995.

Knippel, Charles T. *The Twelve Steps: The Church's Challenge and Opportunity*. St. Louis: CPH, 1994.

Miller, Keith. *Sin: Overcoming the Ultimate Deadly Addiction*. San Francisco: Harper and Row, Publishers, 1987.

Schaef, Anne Wilson. *Codependence Misunderstood—Mistreated*. San Francisco: Harper and Row, Publishers, 1986.

_____. *Escape from Intimacy: The Pseudo-Relationship Addictions*. San Francisco: Harper and Row, Publishers, 1989.

_____. *When Society Becomes an Addict*. San Francisco: Harper and Row, Publishers, 1987.

Schaef, Anne Wilson and Fassel, Diane. *The Addictive Organization*. San Francisco: Harper & Row, Publishers, 1988.

Wegscheider-Cruse, Sharon. *The Miracle of Recovery: Healing Addicts, Adult Children, and Co-Dependents*. Deerfield Beach, FL: Health Communications, 1989.

Woititz, Janet G. *Adult Children of Alcoholics*. Pompano Beach, FL: Health Communication, Inc. 1983.